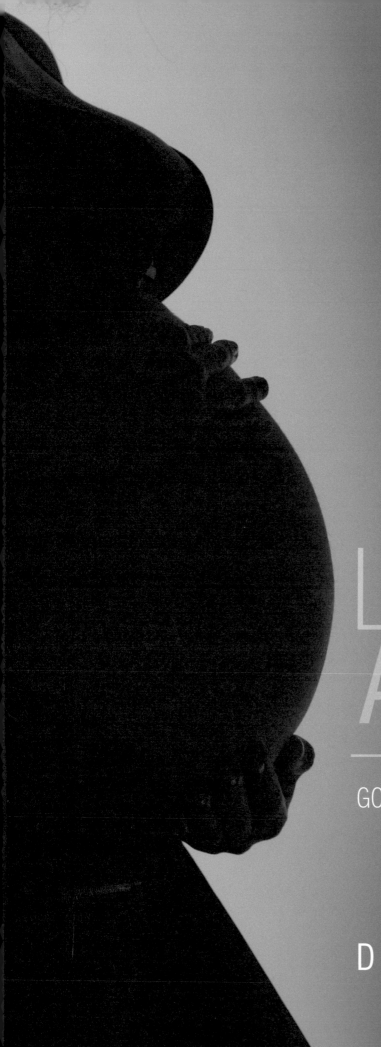

LEAVE ALIVE!

GOODBYE DOMESTIC VIOLENCE

DANETTE MAHABEER

AuthorHouse™
1663 Liberty Drive
Bloomington, IN 47403
www.authorhouse.com
Phone: 1 (800) 839-8640

Scripture taken from The Holy Bible, King James Version. Public Domain

Scripture quotations marked NKJV are taken from the New King James Version. Copyright
© 1982 by Thomas Nelson, Inc. Used by permission. All rights reserved.

Scripture quotations marked NIV are taken from the Holy Bible, New International Version®. NIV®. Copyright ©
1973, 1978, 1984 by International Bible Society. Used by permission of Zondervan. All rights reserved. [Biblica]

Published by AuthorHouse 02/07/2019

ISBN: 978-1-5462-7944-0 (sc)
ISBN: 978-1-5462-7943-3 (e)

Library of Congress Control Number: 2019901383

Print information available on the last page.

Any people depicted in stock imagery provided by Getty Images are models,
and such images are being used for illustrative purposes only.
Certain stock imagery © Getty Images.

This book is printed on acid-free paper.

Because of the dynamic nature of the Internet, any web addresses or links contained in
this book may have changed since publication and may no longer be valid. The views
expressed in this work are solely those of the author and do not necessarily reflect the views
of the publisher, and the publisher hereby disclaims any responsibility for them.

authorHOUSE®

DEDICATION

This book is dedicated to my mother, who walked away from Domestic Abuse in its early stage, with three young children all under the age of 5, and while I was only 2 months old. Having told us the story over and over as children, why and how she left our father and chose to be a single mother, instead of having us witness her being abused or seeing our father, who was an alcoholic, being abusive to her, has given me all the knowledge and strength that I needed, to both identify and avoid a toxic relationship as an adult. It has also taught me to walk away from anything or anyone that devalues my worth.

I also dedicate this book to my daughter Soheila, who has given me a reason to live and has motivated and inspired me every single day of my life. This book is designed to be a constant reminder for her, to never settle for less than she truly deserves and to always believe in herself.

I pray, that this book and the way she is being raised, will be a continuous guide throughout her adult life, to easily Identify, avoid and walk away from absolutely any form of toxic relationship or abuse.

I also extend the dedication of this book, to anyone who has experienced Domestic Abuse in the past, but was able to find the strength, courage and bravery to **'Leave Alive'**.

To those who are currently a victim of Domestic Violence, I pray that a copy of this book will reach your hands in time and speak to your hearts, in gaining the strength, confidence, bravery and courage that it necessitates to **'Leave Alive'** before it is too late.

ACKNOWLEDGEMENT

First and foremost, I want to acknowledge and thank the head of my life, my Heavenly Father Jesus Christ, for having kept his hands on me and who has brought me through many stormy seas, but has never once left or forsaken me. I thank him for his mercies, forgiveness, guidance, protection and his indescribable and unexplainable love towards me on a daily basis.

I extend sincere gratitude to my loving mother, who has always been my back bone and support system throughout my entire life and has been there for me through thick and thin.

I thank my family for being very supportive and for all their love, concern, prayers and encouragement on a daily basis.

I would also like to thank my Pastor and the entire church family, who fervently pray for me and my family daily. Thank you for loving and accepting us with open arms into the family of God.

CONTENTS

INTRODUCTION

Although I was raised well and was constantly reminded of my mother's encounter with Domestic Violence, things do happen and sometimes it is very hard for one to realize that someone so kind could quickly become such a brutal person. I was always aware of the signs to look for in identifying a toxic relationship or person, and even how to avoid being involved in one or with one. However, unforeseen and uncontrollable events will somehow still inevitably affect our lives. The biggest sign that is often overlooked in toxic relationships, is the obligatory force of having to make long term and life changing decisions instantaneously. Rushing in, defeats the purpose of getting to know the other person well. This sudden decision will affect your thought process, and your conclusion would have perhaps been different, if adequate time was given or taken to better analyze and evaluate the affair as well as the individual, over a period of time, during courtship.

Victims of Domestic Violence are not labelled as weak or foolish. These individuals are normally strong, intelligent, smart, confident and successful. Anyone can become a victim of abuse or get caught in this deceiving trap. As a matter of fact, abusers prey on those who are considered to be successful and strong, as their intention is to overwhelm and stress their victims in becoming weak and helpless, which make them feel confident about themselves and feel that they have accomplished power and control over their victims.

You feel as though, it had been the best thing to have ever happened to you. You feel like you cannot let this great escapade bypass you. Finally, a dream come true or a fairy tale "happily ever after" story, as presumed. You become excited because you are well treated or should I say at first. Yes, I just said "at first", because that's exactly how they typically start off. Abusers are great pretenders, who work nonstop until they impress you. Victims generally get caught in these deceiving traps, due to the kindness and warmth that abusers portray in the beginning, which is normally very convincing and promising. But before you know it, you find yourself in a toxic relationship, which then quickly escalates into Domestic Violence. If observed, the signs will be evident and eventually you must conduct some self-analyzation and self-preservation, and take action, in order to avoid staying in an abusive relationship and exiting smartly and safely.

As a Women Advocate and a Domestic Violence Activist, I was inspired to write and publish this book, aspiring that, it will help someone today and save someone's life tomorrow.

I hope, whoever reads this book, will find something advantageous from it and will gain strength, courage, wisdom, hope and support, in taking the next step toward ending the abuse, **"Leave Alive"** and staying safe.

I pray that God will supply you with his guidance, strength and peace and remind you of his unconditional love for you daily. May God Bless You All.

RAISING WARRIORS

Children live what they learn and learn what they live. If a child is taught how to overcome obstacles and challenges, with supervision, yet very minimal assistance, he or she will develop inner strength and will therefore realize that giving up is never an option. If parents and guardians do too much for their children, they will not learn how to be independent and strong for themselves. They will grow up believing that, they must always rely on someone else, just about anyone who may seem to be a shoulder they think they can lean on. Don't get me wrong, we all need a shoulder to lean on from time to time, but let's reflect on the old saying: You give a man a fish, you feed him for a day, but if you teach him how to fish, you feed him for life. Now let's apply this same analogy to how we raise our children. If a child fails at solving a puzzle piece and quickly becomes frustrated, and his parents then put the puzzle together for him to appease his frustration, he will always have an expectation, that if he gets frustrated, he does not have to try too hard because someone else can figure it out for him. He will become an adult who is dependent. However, parents who guide their children, while providing support and minimal involvement, instead of putting it together for them, will experience greater results in their children, who will then evolve into independent and confident adults.

The term 'warrior', is defined as a brave fighter. A fighter is typically considered an opponent, and in the minds of most, are automatically categorized as a victor. To fight, one has to gain courage and strength to stand up to an opponent. In order for one to be able to stand up to a challenger, he or she must first identify what exactly they are opposing to and if it is worth fighting for.

Learning and identifying the difference between what is worth fighting for, in comparison to what is not, is the first step to take, before essentially putting up a fight. It is always best to walk away from the things that are not worth fighting for. This does not mean that you have lost nor does it mean that you are weak. What this truly means is that, you know your worth and you can easily determine and analyze, if a certain situation is worth the fight or not. Walking away from a situation, signifies that you are strong enough to do so, because it is not worth your time and energy. "Don't be a fighter for nothing; be a fighter for something worth fighting for". After you have identified your worth, it will be easier for you to hand-pick your battles accordingly.

Raising your children to become warriors take courage, bravery and strength. This courage, bravery and strength, must first be seen and exerted in the person, whom they are emulating and are hoping to extract those characteristics and traits from. Therefore, if you are to effectively raise up warriors, you must first exert the traits of a warrior.

Parents are considered the first role models for their children. A two year old child will routinely kneel down beside his or her mother, every time she kneels down to pray. Although, as your child grows, he or she will definitely have other forms of influence, it is however normal, for your child to imitate you.

Giving up is never an option. Walking away, is better than fighting an undeserving battle. Never let your children grow up believing that crying is a sign of weakness. Crying allows one, to empty the spaces filled with emotional distress and make it clear for new hope and strength.

How do you feel when you are overwhelmed with a lot of emotional pain? Do you feel a sense of relief or do you feel weighed down? How do you feel after crying about your devastating emotional distresses? Do you feel relieved? Do you feel stronger and hopeful?

Crying improves your mood and helps you to recover from grief. There is nothing wrong with crying. The weakest persons are those who do not cry or think that crying is a form of weakness. If your child cries after losing a football game, hug him and encourage him, instead of telling him to be a man about it and that boys don't cry. Encourage him, to believe in himself and to believe that he can aim to win again. Support and comfort him. The results will be unbelievable.

Many adults today, who suffer from depression, are affected by the fact that they never felt supported or encouraged as children, by the most important people in their lives.

Nay, in all these things we are more than conquerors through him that loved us.

Romans 8:37
KJV

ENCOURAGING CONFIDENCE

If a child is commended, he will learn to be confident. Admiration, is when you tell your child what you like or appreciate about his or her behavior. By using applause, you are showing your children how to think and talk positively about themselves. Allow your children to make decisions, even from a very tender age. As parents, guide them with decision making and provide them with options to choose from, so that they do not overdo it or always try to run the show.

Nurture your children's special interests. Expose them to a wide variety of activities, and encourage them to find something they really love. As parents, try to promote problem solving with your children. Children are confident, when they are able to negotiate getting what they want or have an input in the final decision process. Look for ways to help others and exert those characteristics. Your children will shadow you. When children feel like they are making a difference, they feel more confident about themselves. Give them responsibilities within the household and allow them to assist with other small projects. Let them feel involved and important. Encourage confidence, by talking to your child about you, your spouse and even careers. Never try to lower your children's expectations. Instead, provide them with options, which will make them believe that you have their best interest at heart.

The most confident adults today are those who were raised with acclamations and those who had great role models. As adults, surround yourselves with other confident individuals and people with mutual interests. Extract from them positively and apply it to your life, while boosting your own confidence. Eat healthy and exercise regularly, as this also helps in reducing stress levels and helps to boost confidence. Engage in activities that you enjoy and pamper yourself from time to time. Surround yourself with people who compliments, encourages and motivates you constantly.

Let your light so shine before men, that they may see your good works, and glorify your Father which is in heaven.

Matthew 5:16
KJV

EMBRACING DIFFERENCES
AND PERSONALITIES

Being raised in a diverse society, can impact either positively or negatively on one's life and beliefs. This is determined by what is being promoted by the people around us. There are different races, colors, religions and cultures, which we are all surrounded by. How do we embrace each of them? We simply embrace based on our beliefs. The word 'embrace', is defined as accepting or supporting a belief, theory or change, willingly and enthusiastically. The word 'belief', is defined as an acceptance that a statement is true or that something exists. It is further extended to having faith, trust or confidence in someone or something. Again, how do we embrace these differences that surround us? It starts by first believing in Jesus Christ and that his indescribable, unexplainable and unconditional love, has been extended to every one of us equally. Therefore, love has to be part of your belief and we must embrace with love.

For God so loved the world, that he gave his only begotten son, that whosoever believeth in him should not perish, but have everlasting life.

John 3:16
KJV

It doesn't matter what the color of one's skin is or the religion they choose, God's greatest desire for us is to love one another and to love our neighbors as ourselves. If you love someone or something, you embrace it dearly. Therefore, despite someone's classified differences and personalities, we must always extend love. We know and feel love, by the way we are treated and by the way we also treat others in return.

Ensure that your children feel loved and are embraced by you on a daily basis, because this is where it all starts. You have a responsibility to teach and practice love toward your children. Show love to everyone around you and everyone you come in contact with, and your children will learn to love others and embrace them, despite their differences and personalities. Self-love is very important and that starts with the amount of love that they themselves are surrounded by.

We all have different personalities and God made us in his own image. We are unique and was made to be different. Everyone has a different finger print. Some people have blue eyes, while some have brown eyes. The same way, we were created to have different personalities. Some people are outspoken, while others are shy. Despite what someone else's characters, traits, opinions or beliefs are, we should love and embrace them. Learn to love and to surround yourself with love. Love is gentle and kind. Surround yourself with people that embrace you, love you and accept you for who you are, without trying to change you into who they want you to be. Surround yourself with people, who allow you to be your true self.

> *If a man say, I love God, and hateth his brother, he is a Liar: for he that loveth not his brother whom he hath seen, how can he love God whom he hath not seen?*

> *1 John 4:20*
> *KJV*

BUILDING SELF-ESTEEM

Self-esteem is defined as confidence in one's own worth or abilities, and having self-respect. Children who grow up feeling insecure, lonely or lacking support, are more likely to be targets of sexual and domestic abuse.

Building self-esteem, starts from raising your children into believers. Every child is different, but children all learn by examples. They see what parents do and what they say. Be kind to your children, motivate them and inspire them. Self-esteem and confidence work hand in hand, since self-esteem is confidence in one's self and confidence is a feeling of self-assurance or believing in one's self.

If children are raised to have high self-esteem, they will become successful and confident adults, acknowledging self-worth and exercising self-love. Celebrate successes and learn from failures. When you are proud of your children, let them know. When they have fallen short of a goal, help them to work on it until they are successful. Children who are supported by parents, normally grow into adults who also learn to celebrate their own success and the success of their own children; and will also learn from their failures, instead of losing courage or confidence.

Learn to be a listener. Listen to your children and what they have to say. Let their voices be heard. Teach them to speak up. Engage them in conversations and let them feel that you have interest in what they have to say. Children who do not speak up or get the chance to express themselves freely, are typically the children who experience bully in school and by peers, and who eventually grow into adults who become victims of Domestic Violence and other forms of abuse. Your interest in your children will inspire them and they will become confident adults. Allow your children to make choices. Giving your children options and allowing them to choose one, will help them to feel empowered and independent. Independent children turn into independent adults. Children with high self-esteem, will grow into adults with high self-esteem.

When you value yourself and have a high self-esteem, you will feel worthwhile and confident. It will be easier for you then, as an adult, to identify a very good relationship versus a toxic relationship and the decisions which are more suitable to make in each of these situations.

Strength and honor are her clothing; and she shall rejoice in time to come.

Proverbs 31:25
KJV

KNOWING YOUR WORTH
(SELF-LOVE & SELF-ACCEPTANCE)

What comes to mind, when you think of the word "worth"? You should immediately think of value. Worth is defined as, the level at which someone or something deserves to be valued or rated. How does one identify their worth? Before being able to do so, one must first know and be able to recognize self-love and self-acceptance.

This starts from childhood and parents play a huge role, in ensuring that their children know their worth, feel loved and feel accepted. Children who are raised feeling unloved, unaccepted or unworthy by their parents - the ones they least expect it from, will eventually grow into adults feeling the same way. Adults who feel unloved, unaccepted or unworthy, are typically the ones who end up staying in abusive and toxic relationships. This is because, they are trying to feel accepted and they do not know what love is or how it feels to be genuinely loved, so they settle for whatever they get and from just about anyone, who gives them some attention. They are vulnerable and customarily suffer from having very low self-esteem.

Self-love starts with parents praising their children when deserved and showing them love daily. Self-acceptance involves self-understanding and awareness of one's strength and weaknesses. If your child can identify his or her strengths and weaknesses, from a tender age, with the support of their parents, they will learn self-acceptance. Self-acceptance also has to do with being comfortable in your own skin. Therefore, parents should ensure that from a very tender age, their children understand that it is okay to look and be different. Help them to identify their strengths and help them to work on their weaknesses, but to also understand that everyone has weaknesses and strengths. Always compliment your child, by telling him or her that they are beautiful. Help them to become the adult who acknowledges self-acceptance. Love your children and let them know you do by your actions. A child that grows with love will always possess self-love and will learn to love others in return.

Knowing and identifying your worth, as an adult, is very important and will help you to choose wisely. Possessing a positive and high self-esteem, are key factors in knowing your worth. You will recognize the difference you make and your values. Be clear about your values and know your boundaries. These very important attributes will help you in identifying what is acceptable and what is not. It will be easier for you to set rules, on how you want to be treated and spoken to, and will speak up when necessary. This kind of attitude will be demonstrated not only for a relationship, but also applies to a job, a boss, colleagues, friends and other family members. People overall, will treat you in the way you allow them to, based on the way you carry yourself and the attributes you portray. Believe that you are good enough and walk away from anything or anyone that does not appreciate or value your worth. Never settle for less. The way in which you also treat others says a lot about you and who you are. Therefore, if people observe that you are respectful and kind to others, they will realize that they too have no choice, but to respect you and demonstrate kindness to you.

Be aware of the kind of relationships that you get involved in. Observe the way in which you are spoken to and treated by this person. Does this person respect you, listen to you and is kind to you? Does he or she show you appreciation and spend quality time with you and enjoy being around you? When there is a disagreement, how is it handled? Does it escalate into a quarrel or fight? Are you being blamed? Do you find yourself always apologizing or always trying to make things right? Do you feel like you are walking on eggshells, or that everything you say or do causes a problem?

Well, if this is you, or you feel that you are currently in a similar situation, then it is time for you to immediately revisit your self-worth and values. Do you allow this person to talk down to you or do you speak up when necessary? Revisiting your self-worth and values will remind you of who you are and what you deserve. Remember, what you allow, is what will continue. Again, never settle for less than you truly deserve, and you deserve the very best and nothing less. Abusers tend to prey on stronger individuals, because it seems more of a challenge to them, to aim at transforming a confident person with high self-esteem into a weaker person, who will eventually suffer from low self-esteem, due to the effect they will have on them in the long run. Not because abusers tend to prey more on stronger individuals, does not mean that persons who suffer from low self-esteem will be exempted from being abused. Abusers will abuse who ever allows them to, whether you are confident or timid.

Remind yourself that you deserve the very best and nothing less. You have learnt to love yourself so do not allow or expect anything less from anyone. Be with someone, who sees and appreciates your values. When you are free from crippling fear of abandonment, you will feel free to speak up. Don't be afraid to ask for what you want and need, and truly deserve. Always stand up for what you believe in, and that is, believing in yourself. Learn to walk away from toxic relationships and friendships. Find ways to improve your self-worth on a daily basis, and enhance your self-love and self-acceptance by creating new interests and doing the things that truly makes you happy.

For no man ever yet hated his own flesh; but nourisheth and cherisheth it, even as the Lord the church.

Ephesians 5:29
KJV

IDENTIFYING TOXIC RELATIONSHIPS

Identifying a toxic relationship will be easier, when one has already recognized his or her worth and values. If as parents, we stay in toxic relationships, then we must expect that our children will grow into adults, believing that it is okay to also stay in one. This is unacceptable. If a boy is raised in a household where he sees his father hitting his mother or bullying her, he will grow up believing that it is okay to behave in the same manner as his father, and thinking that it is also okay for him to hit a woman. If a girl witness the very same setting, she will grow up, thinking that it is okay for a man to hit her and that it is okay for her to stay, believing that it is normal.

There are numerous signs to look for, when identifying a toxic relationship; and if at any time these signs become evident, it is time for you to take actions and remove yourself from that atmosphere. No relationship is perfect. Always keep God in the center of your marriage. Pray and consult him and he will guide your way. You cannot change another person. They have to want to change and make efforts toward doing so. Therefore, if these signs continue or multiply, then it is time to free yourself from that environment and walk away from that relationship.

A good relationship, will make you feel secured, respected, cared for and happy, and will allow you to be yourself. On the other hand, a toxic relationship, will make you feel distressed, anxious, and depleted. It is time to re-evaluate your relationship, if you are always mentally, physically and emotionally drained, instead of feeling happy and loved. If your atmosphere is filled with constant anger and hostility, then the truth is, you are in an unhealthy relationship. Hostility will drive fear into you and cause you to feel unsafe. If your partner always criticize you, instead of complimenting you, and is always trying to make you feel bad about yourself, you are in a toxic relationship. If your partner always find fault, instead of seeing the good in the situation, this will eventually cause you to lose interest and later suffer from low self-esteem.

It is almost impossible for anything positive to come out of a relationship filled with negativity. A negative person, will find a problem to every solution and a fault instead of a compliment. Even when it is well deserved, they can't help themselves from being a vibe killer and a critic. A toxic relationship, always have a one sided and controlling partner, who thinks that everything must always go his or her way with no exceptions whatsoever. They never like to compromise and always believe that their idea or their way is always a better choice than yours. If you constantly feel like nothing you do is ever done right and is always being blamed for everything, then you are in a toxic relationship.

God's greatest desire for us is to love and be loved. Therefore, if a relationship makes you feel unloved, uncomfortable or feel that you can never be your true self, then it is time for some re-examination. If you find yourself changing your opinions or decisions to please someone else, you are in a toxic and damaging relationship, which will soon cause you to lose yourself.

Although you may have already recognized your worth, being in a relationship with someone who doesn't acknowledge your worth, will change the way you feel about yourself, causing you to compromise your values eventually.

If a relationship is lacking communication and understanding, it will soon deteriorate and fade. If every conversation turns into an argument or quarrel, then you are in a toxic relationship.

Love suffers long and is kind; love does not envy; love does not parade itself, is not puffed up; does not behave rudely, does not seek its own, is not provoked, thinks no evil; does not rejoice in iniquity, but rejoices in the truth; bears all things, believes all things, hopes all things, endures all things.

1 Corinthians 13:4-7
NKJV

AVOIDING TOXIC RELATIONSHIPS

Toxic relationships may take many different forms. While most toxic relationships and abusers start off being very interesting and promising, it will quickly change, if you pay close attention. Having identified the signs to look for in a toxic relationship or person, will help you to avoid being in one or with one. It is harder to get out of a toxic relationship or to walk away from a toxic person, than it is to avoid getting fooled by one.

Learning how to quickly recognize psychological disorders, which are typically identified in toxic relationships and toxic individuals, will help you in avoiding one. The best time to identify a toxic relationship or person, is normally during courtship. Doing so during this period, will help you to avoid being involved in one or with one.

Pay close attention to the signs. How do you feel when you are around this person? Keep in mind, abusers are great pretenders, who will quickly convince you that they are the right one for you. Avoid any relationship that moves too fast and hurries or forces you to make long term decisions instantaneously. A toxic person cannot hide his or her personality and behavior for too long, and will therefore force you into making sudden, yet binding decisions. Be very careful.

A toxic person can be described as a jealous and judgmental person, which typically comes off as criticism or gossip. They normally have very low self-esteem and little or no confidence; so in order for them to feel better about themselves, they put down other people. They see what's wrong in everyone else, and believe that everyone is lacking something in one way or another. They are negative and find fault with everything and everyone. They make excuses and find a problem for every solution.

A relationship is toxic, when one person is running the show. We should never feel powerless or trapped. Each partner should feel energized and complete. Each person should still feel free to be themselves, and not having to change everything about them to please their partner.

Trust is the foundation of a healthy relationship. If trust is broken, forgiveness and reconciliation cannot begin, until the truth is told. Therefore, if a person is dishonest and frequently lies to you, avoid building a relationship with them. This is one of the first signs to look for, in identifying a toxic person, who is going to be the main contributor to a toxic relationship. Avoid it at all cost. It will save you time and energy in the long run. If you are able to identify a negative and toxic person, you are more than likely able to avoid a toxic relationship. Avoid persons who are dishonest, demanding, controlling, aggressive and judgmental.

Avoid persons who never own up to their mistakes or admit their wrongs. Those who never take responsibility for their actions, are also to be avoided at all cost.

Toxicity is contagious and insidious, and even those who are kind can be affected. When avoiding a toxic relationship, start by creating distance instead of an immediate separation, in order to circumvent any form of retaliation which may follow. This rule and method is advised for both courtship and for an active serious relationship. After these signs are observed and become evident, take actions cautiously.

If you are trapped in a toxic relationship and have identified and recognized one or more of the mentioned signs, in your current relationship, then it is time for you to seek help, in order to get out safely.

> *Walk with the wise and become wise, for a companion of fools suffers harm.*

Proverbs 13:20
NIV

LIVE TO LOVE, NOT LOVE TO DEATH

Often times, a lover may use the expression "I love you to death", referring to their partner. What exactly does this saying mean? What exactly do they mean, when they use this phrase? Are they referring to the "till death do us part" that the bible accentuates, or are they referring to the indication of "If I can't have you, no one else can or will".

The "till death do us part" that the bible speaks of, is referring to God's desire for his people: to love, to cherish and honor your husband or wife. God wants us to keep our promises, just as he keeps his promises to us. However, the "I love you to death" on the other hand, can sometimes be a very dangerous sign and way of expression. Stating that you love someone to death is inconspicuously signifying, that you love them till they die. The "till death do us part" phrase however, is referring to any of the two parties being separated by death, rather than just the person you love dying. Any of the two can die at any time, and it means that until then, your duties and responsibilities are to honor, love and cherish that person while being together and alive. Live to love the person, not love them to death, but instead, as the word of God commands "Till death do us part".

Nevertheless let every one of you in particular so love his wife even as himself; and the wife see that she reverence her husband.

Ephesians 5:33
KJV

Be honest to your partner and be with someone who is going to be honest to you as well. Love your husbands and wives, with the love of God. Be gentle, be kind, honor and cherish that person for the rest of your life; for as long as you both shall live. There you have it! That's the kind of "till death do us part" that we should practice, and that the bible speaks about; not the kind that consists of jealousy, egotism, selfishness, anger and hate. Show your love with your actions. If you notice that your partner constantly tells you he or she loves you, but his or her actions are contradictory to that phrase, then something is wrong. Words must match actions and not be the other way around. There has to be communication, understanding and collaboration. Compromising plays a huge factor in a successful marriage and partnership.

Prayer must be a key part of your life and is very essential in every successful marriage. There will be problems and differences from time to time; that's a part of every relationship. However, the way in which they are dealt with, determines the attainment of your relationship. Other issues such as financial issues and other family related issues can and may cause a strain on your marriage but nothing beats prayer, and having a spouse, who is mutually connected to God as you are, does make things calmer and healthier. Pray together and ask for God's divine intervention. Only he alone is able to step in and fix our complications.

Trust in the Lord with all thine heart; and lean not unto thine own understanding. In all thy ways acknowledge him, and he shall direct thy paths.

Proverbs 3:5-6
KJV

EXERCISING COURAGE AND BRAVERY

Courage is defined as strength in the face of pain or grief. It is also the ability to do something that frightens one. Bravery is defined as courageous behavior or character. Bravery is the ability to confront pain, danger or even attempts of intimidation, without any feeling of fear. While on the other hand, courage is the ability to undertake an overwhelming difficulty or pain, despite the eminent and unavoidable presence of fear. Through exercising both courage and fear, one is expressing fearlessness, boldness, intrepidity and dauntlessness. During the phase of our grief, difficulty or pain, it is normal and human like for us to feel and suffer from fear to some extent, however, it is definitely our inner strength, which we must rely and depend on, in order to effectively be able to exercise courage and bravery.

The bible speaks of an inimitable and one of a kind strength, which is given by and comes only from God. That strength, will give you the courage and bravery it will require to break silence, stand up for what you believe in and take the necessary actions, after carefully evaluating your current dilemma.

God is our refuge and strength, a very present help in trouble.

Psalm 46:1
KJV

Whatever the circumstance may be, courage and bravery are customarily required, when making certain tough decisions, especially while feeling overwhelmed with difficulty or facing danger. Sometimes we really have no other choice, but to be valiant, audacious and courageous. An abuser, a bully or a toxic person, does not expect you to be bold or fearless, because they always self-assuredly feel powerful, authoritative, manipulative and in control. Consequently, standing up for yourself and putting a stop to the things that are affecting or endangering you, will unquestionably change the game plan. Often times, it confuse abusers and bullies, when such bravery and courageousness is demonstrated, by one whom they presume should have been the opposite. Therefore, one still has to be very vigilant, as the loss of control may cause an abuser or bully to become very aggressive, retaliatory and dangerous. At this point, the abuser only sees you as being very disobedient and recalcitrant, for portraying such bravery, boldness and courage. However, standing up and speaking up is always the better option.

Being vulnerable, susceptible and defenseless, only give abusers more power and control over you and the overall existing situation; and that's exactly what they want and enjoy. Exercising courage and bravery, means that you now have some very important and serious decisions and actions to make and take, as things may possibly go down south from this point onward. Do not let that scare you or let it stop you from making what is considered a crucial decision. In order to make the next important move, toward completely putting a stop to the abuse, this significant phase of **"Exercising Courage and Bravery"**, has to first be confronted, established and demonstrated. This compulsory step has been proven to enhance self-reliance, in preparing victims to be more vigorous, when confronting and challenging the next indispensable phase in order to end the Domestic Abuse or any other form of Abuse or Bullying that one may be currently enduring.

Be strong and of good courage, fear not, nor be afraid of them: for the Lord thy God, he it is that doth go

with thee; he will not fail thee, nor forsake thee.

Deuteronomy 31:6
KJV

BREAKING SILENCE

Having developed the courage and bravery that it necessitates to end an abuse, the next phase is **"Breaking Silence"**. This means, that you will no longer keep this abuse a secret between just you and the abuser. This is where and when you will have to now confide in someone else and get the help and resources that you will need, in order to safely get out of an abusive relationship or to end any other forms of abuse, which you may be experiencing. No form of abuse or bullying should ever be kept a secret. Confide in a trustworthy family member or friend, speak to an Advocacy Center in your area and report the abuse and the abuser to your local Police Department. Speak up and speak out.

The average victims are usually terrified to report the abuse and their abuser, and most often times keep it a secret, because of feeling ashamed, distressed and threatened. Victims typically feel afraid of their abuser and the anticipated retaliatory conduct that the abuser will portray, after finding out that the victim has reported the abuse. This predicted revengeful behavior that is being referred to, often times have a very dangerous effect on the victim, and can make matters worse, if this step is not approached with caution and with the necessary resources that are readily available to assist victims in safely ending abuse.

If a victim confides in you about being abused, you too, the by-stander, have a responsibility to also break the silence. Do not keep the abuse a secret between you and the victim. Although it may also be scary for you, you too have to quickly gain the courage and bravery, which is required to break silence. Abuse is no secret. It is a killer and a disease, which has been widely spread worldwide and has become frequent in our communities today. It should not be overlooked, avoided or underestimated. The effect is has on our society is lethal.

It is always very difficult for a victim to open up about being abused, due to the fear and trauma they are currently enduring and anticipate. Filing police reports about an abuse and elaborating on the circumstance, even to an Advocacy Center or Counselor, can be a very difficult phase for victims, because they have to ultimately relive the abuse, by expounding and explaining all the details of each event, while still experiencing fear, harassment and trauma at the same time. However, as hard as it may be for a victim, the smartest thing to do, is to break the silence. This phase will encourage and strengthen victims, who sequentially followed all the previous phases. The support that victims receive from family members, friends and Advocacy Centers after **"Breaking Silence"**, is remarkable. No one will know, unless you tell them. Having broken the silence, Advocacy Centers are readily available and prepared to provide victims with the necessary information, support and resources, which will help them in whatever phase of Domestic Abuse they are currently in or challenged with; and with other forms of abuse as well. There are various Advocacy Centers available in your area for various types of abuse. Find the ones that are designed to better assist you and the type of abuse that you are experiencing. This phase, will allow you to realize that you are not alone and that if you speak up and let someone know about the abuse you are experiencing, there is always help, support and resources readily available to you.

It is very important to know the signs to look for in an abusive relationship and traits in an abusive person. Some people do not know that they are experiencing abuse, because they often times do not even know what abuse feels or looks like; and may think that it is normal to be treated in that manner. All types of abuse exist in a system of power and control. Abusers victimize, in order to gain power and to feel that they are in control of their victims.

Although this book is primarily focused on, addressing the issues of Domestic Violence and providing support and advice in ending Domestic Abuse, it is very important that we become aware of all the other types of existing Abuse and Bullying, that our society is challenged with daily. The forms of Abuse include but is not limited to: Mental, Emotional, Verbal, Financial, Physical, Sexual, Psychological and of course Domestic Abuse. Bullying is also considered a type of abuse and can therefore take various forms as well. This includes but is not limited to: Cyberbully, Verbal, Direct, Indirect, Emotional and Physical Bullying. No form of Abuse or Bullying should ever be tolerated, accepted or become a norm for our society and community. Some of the mutual signs to look for in all forms of Abuse and Bullying may include but not limited to: manipulation, threats, injury or pain, control, lies, jealousy, isolation and anything that hurts the victim, physically or emotionally. Regardless of the type of abuse a victim may be experiencing, family members of the victim are also affected.

If you suspect that a family member, friend, neighbor or co-worker is being abused, try to find out more, by asking questions, which will assure the victim that you sincerely care and is genuinely concerned and want to help. Give a listening ear and be very attentive to the details. Remember, silence means validation. So if you observe that someone is being abused, it is also your responsibility to break the silence as well. Break Silence on all forms of Abuse and bullying today.

Open thy mouth, judge righteously, and plead the cause of the poor and needy.

Proverbs 31:9
KJV

WALKING AWAY

Walking away, sounds like an easy thing to do or even say, but to be honest, it sometimes can be the hardest thing one has to ever do. It is a very tough decision, which requires strength, boldness, courage, confidence, faith and bravery. For many Domestic Violence victims, their abuser ensures that they are always in control and is normally very manipulative and calculative. Already experiencing fear and anxiety, the victim will be hesitant, to even attempt to take this next step, because they dread what the abuser may do to them, if they leave or attempt to leave. By this time, a victim is usually completely convinced, that the abuser is so powerful, and that they the victim feel so defenseless, vulnerable and often times, feel alone, due to the isolation from family and friends caused by the abuser. This isolation is a trick, which initially separates victims, from those who truly care for them, in order to eliminate the help, support and resources, which would have been available to them otherwise. Abusers tend to pretend, that they are taking care of your every needs, causing you to believe, that there is no need to look anywhere else or do anything else, but is instead only preventing or limiting you from earning and even having control over your own money. Therefore, victims are normally dependent on their abusers and feel that if they leave or walk away, they will have no way out financially. What will I do? Who will pay the bills? How will I take care of myself or the children? Where will we go? These are just some of the questions that most victims find themselves asking, by the time they get to this phase. This was exactly the abuser's goal. They never want you to be or feel independent, because then you will not need them to survive and will gain more confidence and courage when having to walk away. Although, having made it successfully past all the previously mentioned stages, some victims at this time, may still lose courage and experience more or some fear buildup from being drained and exhausted from the constant harassment and manipulation by the abuser, and after asking themselves those questions. Victims sometimes compromise their next move or action, after re-evaluating and asking themselves those questions, which eventually build up fear of the unknown.

During this phase, victims may struggle with both mixed emotions and with the final decision-making process. In one instance, they may feel ready and prepared to leave, but then in another, they question their tomorrow with lots of "What If". The fear of the unknown is real and can easily cause victims to run back into a shell, giving abusers even more authority and control over the situation.

Victims sometimes find themselves even asking, "Who will want me?" This is because, the victim is already suffering from low self-esteem, caused by the abuser, which is a trick to keep you trapped in the abuse, while losing yourself and your true identity. Abusers will try to convince you, that no one else will love you or want you, and will eventually get you to believe that this is really true. They will put you down and criticize you constantly, which will inevitably have a major effect on your self-esteem and self-identity.

"Wanting to leave, but scared", "wanting to walk away, but how will I survive?" These are the two main reasons, why most victims stay in abusive relationships and sidestep the **"Walking Away"** phase. Fear tied with the lack of self-acceptance and self-love, are the main cause for this. Fear is defined as an unpleasant emotion caused by anticipation or awareness of danger, or an anxious concern.

The truth is, each abusive event will only worsen. So keep in mind your time is winding down. Having broken the silence, this step, although still very difficult, may become easier for a victim to take actions and walk away, knowing that the support they are receiving from family members, friends and Advocacy Centers is genuine and assured. **"Walking Away"** is very hard and can be tempting; if you somehow manage to leave, you may even feel the urge to return to the abuse or the abuser since it is familiar. However, if you managed to walk away but somehow return to the abuser or abusive relationship, the abuser will fear that you will try to leave again, and any sign of attempt will trigger the anger and actions of the abuser. This can become very dangerous and life threatening for the victim. Abusers never want to feel like they have lost control, and any sign of that, will cause them to become revengeful, dangerous and aggressive; and may even lead to life threatening events. Therefore, if you managed to safely walk away, please do not look back. Avoid going back, it will only get worse. Block all temptation to return, and do not be fooled or convinced by the pathetic apologies from the abuser. The truth is, if he hit you once, he is going to do it again and even worse than the first.

How many times have you heard the words "I'm Sorry", even before getting to this phase? Did it get any better or did it get worse? Do you think that going back will make it better or worse? Ask yourself these rhetorical questions and conduct some self-analyzation. Although the answers to these questions are evident, by doing so, it will help to remind you of the nature of the situation, and will help you in gaining the strength and bravery it will take to move on and not look back.

Walking away is life changing. Things may feel weird or unusual at first and for a while, but that's okay. You may even feel lost, confused or traumatized, but walking away should be final, in order to avoid life threatening events. Never display any sign of insinuation or hint to your abuser. Your abuser should never be aware of your planned departure. This is the only secret, which should be tightly kept. Although it is normal for victims to be distraught and very difficult for a victim to act calm, especially during the planning of a departure, it is however very necessary to pretend that way, to avoid letting your abuser suspect your next move.

There are a lot of support groups and available resources, to those who are affected by all forms of abuse. Victims who use or access these important resources and information, tend to benefit positively, and experience better outcome and results in the long run.

But now thus saith the Lord that created thee, O Jacob, and he that formed thee, O Israel, Fear not: for I have redeemed thee, I have called thee by thy name; thou art mine. When thou passest through the waters, I will be with thee; and through the rivers, they shall not overflow thee: when thou walkest through the fire, thou shalt not be burned; neither shall the flame kindle upon thee. For I am the Lord thy God, the Holy One of Israel, thy Savior: I gave Egypt for thy ransom, Ethiopia and Seba for thee.

Isaiah 43:1-3
KJV

STAYING SAFE

Although you may have walked away and may be somewhere safe, there are still some other very important factors to take into consideration, in order to stay safe, after leaving an abuser. **"Staying Safe"** means keeping your current location private and should be kept a secret from not just your abuser, but absolutely anyone, who is capable of compromising your safety, whether persuasively or by just simply being an untrustworthy individual.

Remember, abusers who feel that they have lost control will, automatically become retaliatory and dangerous. You may even need to change your phone number or avoid calls from private or unknown numbers. Keep your location off at all times, to avoid being stalked or trailed. Avoid posting on social media sites, and it is best if you just avoid capturing photos for now. This is to cautiously avoid capturing the name of places, which you may have to frequently visit, in the event, that your phone data is hacked. Report all suspicious behavior or actions of your abuser. Call the emergency police number, if at any time you feel threatened or believe that you are being followed. Get a safe sound personal alarm emergency siren and attach it to your keychain or bag. This will help to draw attention to your location, should someone attempt to attack you. It may also scare off attackers caused by the effect of the alarming sound.

Avoid lonely areas such as, parking garage or dark parking lot, and avoid going to places alone. If it is possible, try to always be accompanied by someone you can trust. Otherwise, always notify someone trustworthy of your whereabouts. Keep a file of all evidence of the abuse, both previously and of any recurrent events, which may have occurred after your departure, accompanied by all police reports that was filed by you.

Create a Safety Plan. This is obligatory. A Safety Plan is a personalized and practical plan, which includes ways to stay safe. This plan can be used by anyone: those who are currently still trapped in an abusive relationship and are planning their departure and for those who have efficaciously escaped one. Ensure to share your Safety Plan with only close friends and family members that are trustworthy, so that in the event you are forced to follow through with your personalized plan, these individuals will be assured, that you are in a safe place and out of the reach of your abuser. This will also preclude putting the people who genuinely care about your safety in a panic.

An effective Safety Plan, will have all of the important information that you need, and is specifically designed to fit each victim's unique situation and circumstance. No two safety plans will necessarily be the same, however, some safety plans may contain mutual information, depending on the nature of the condition. One mutual factor, of any safety plan includes, always having a full tank of gas in your car, in case you have to make an instantaneous move.

When there is a moment of crisis, the brain tends to freeze and may even cause victims to go into a panic. Therefore, although some of the things in your Safety Plan may seem obvious, make sure they are included in your written Safety Plan, in order to avoid making the wrong decisions during a panic. Always keeps your Safety Plan handy, and always try to get familiar with your Safety Plan habitually.

Avoid being predictable. Therefore, during this phase you may want to even avoid visiting the same places such as gas stations, stores or restaurants. You may have to just simply keep a low profile; that's it. No distraction or compromising is allowed during this phase. Stay focus, be alert and stay safe.

Thou art my hiding place; thou shalt preserve me from trouble; thou shalt compass me about with songs of deliverance. Selah.

Psalm 32:7
KJV

FROM VICTIM TO VICTOR

Whether you consider yourself a Victim or a Victor, begins with your mentality, mindset and attitude. We cannot control the things that happen to us in life, but we are able to control how we receive it, how we react to it and how we respond overall. Whether we receive it as a Victim or a Victor and whether we view it as a weakness or a lesson (combined with newly gained strength), all starts with our outlook. It takes strength and courage to become a Victor. Although it is always easier for us to blame the one who has hurt and victimized us, it is better however, to mentally, physically and psychologically transform the situation, by identifying and executing the things that we are able to control and contribute positively to the ill-fated situation.

A Victim feels like they can't succeed, while a Victor feels they must succeed. Again, the difference is analyzed based on our mindset. A Victim focuses on external pressures, while a Victor concentrates on inward confidence and self-reliance. A Victim uses excuses, while a Victor finds a way to keep going. During a tough situation, Victims will just feel bad about themselves, while those who possess a Victor mentality, will find ways to fix the problems as they arise and are able to move on, exerting a positive attitude and energy. Victims accept human nature, while Victors want to fight against it inevitably.

Were you raised as a Victim or a Victor? How are you raising your children today? Are you raising them to be Victims or Victors? Though we are constantly faced with challenges, how do we triumph? What strategies do we use to fight against the issues of life which forces us to stumble and struggle? Do we fight back negatively or positively? How do we react? How do we respond?

The term 'Victim', is defined as one who is subjected to oppression, hardship or mistreatment. What we allow in our lives, is what will continue. A Victor, on the other hand, is defined as a person who defeats an opponent in a battle. Being victimized is a battle. The term 'battle' is defined as a fight or struggle, tenaciously to achieve or resist something. The operative word is 'resist'. This is where a Victor mindset is stimulated. Confront your situation with faith and courage, and challenge your battles.

The bible speaks of a specific kind of resistance, that is applicable in any situation or battles, which we may encounter in this world. It also expounds on the fact that we will be faced with these battles and challenges in our lives, but it also offers a lot of guide and direction, on how to triumph and be victorious.

Submit yourselves therefore to God. Resist the devil, and he will flee from you.

James 4:7
KJV

Struggles affect us at random and come in all forms and sizes. Fear, persecution and worries can easily take over our thoughts. God tells us that we will face trials, but he reminds us that we are not alone and we should not lose hope. God has called us to be overcomers and conquerors. Be encouraged. Apply the word of God to your daily life, as well as your situations and challenges. Uplift your spirit and mind, and be reminded, that God fights our battles for us and on our behalf, and all we need to do is to take it to him in prayer, and allow him to guide us daily. We also have a role to play, as God helps those who help themselves. We can start helping ourselves today, by converting our mindset from being that of a Victim to effectively actuating our purpose, as God has called us to be conquerors and overcomers. Stand up for what you believe in and learn to start fighting your battles with the word of God, and enhance your prayer life, while allowing God to take care of the rest for you.

For the Lord your God is he that goeth with you, to fight for you against your enemies, to save you.

Deuteronomy 20:4
KJV

CULTIVATING THE ADVOCATE IN YOU

Becoming an Advocate of any form, requires interest, awareness and passion. A person who has been victimized in the past, can easily relate to victims who are currently experiencing the same form of abuse. Although becoming an Advocate, may be considered a very challenging mission for some survivors, they are considered the most effective Activists, because they are devoted and enthused to help other victims become survivors like themselves. With the hope of ending abuse of all kinds in our society today, that are rapidly increasing and affecting our communities daily, survivors are very passionate in volunteering in these areas. Survivors are already aware of the signs to pinpoint and look for in a comparable abusive situation, and they have already gained some knowledge on the issue and the actions to take, since they have previously undergone the stages of support, from other Advocates and resource centers of the same kind, that assisted them in becoming Survivors today.

On the other hand however, anyone can become an Advocate, having established the self-developed passion, interest, awareness and proper training that it requires. Some Advocates, were never victims, however, a loved one was victimized, and that may also inspire individuals to become passionate Advocates. In our Society and communities today, these crimes of abuse, have become so widespread and domineering; therefore, the need for Advocates are continuously multiplying.

If you have ever thought of becoming an Advocate, for any type of the ever-increasing abuse, which is affecting our society and communities today, please do not hesitate. If you have developed a passion for the issue, then pursue it. God has a purpose for all of us and sometimes, in order to actuate that purpose, we must first experience some challenges and have gained the knowledge, strength and courage, that it will require for us to be effective in our purpose. Unquestionably, we must pray about it and ask God to guide us in stimulating our purpose.

For God is not unrighteous to forget your work and labor of love, which ye have shewed towards his name, in that ye have ministered to the saints, and do minister.

Hebrews 6:10
KJV

SHE IS ALIVE TODAY BECAUSE
(A POEM FOR BATTERED WOMEN)

She is alive today, because she did not stay in the abuse. Although it was very hard for her to walk away, she found the strength and courage to leave alive. She is alive today, because she did not stay.

Though he apologized and brought her flowers and gifts every time he hit her, she is alive today, because she did not stay. He said he was sorry and she believed him every time, but the abuse only got worse and she was terrified.

She could have died. But thank God, she is alive today, because she finally gained the strength, courage and bravery that she needed to walk away.

Be brave, avoid the grave.

Walk away. Do not stay another day!

Written by: Danette Mahabeer

A LETTER TO MY DAUGHTER

Dear Soheila,

    I am very blessed and grateful to call you my child. You bring me so much joy, love and happiness. You have taught me patience and kindness. You are a masterpiece. You are loved. God loves you and just know that I love you too with all my heart. You are very unique. There is no one else in this world like you; always remember that.

Please do not allow anyone to define who you are or who you should be. You will make mistakes, and that's okay. Learn from those mistakes and move onward. Stand up for what is right, even when it is hard. Please do not allow violence against you, in neither actions nor words. Please do not allow anyone or anything to belittle you or challenge your confidence. Do not compromise your worth. Please stand up for yourself and always remember, you are strong and confident. Do not allow anyone or anything to change the true you.

Allow God to always be the center of your life and always acknowledge him in order to be appropriately guided by his will and purpose for your life. I will always be here for you. I will always support you and protect you. I believe in you and in your abilities.

However, if I can't be there for you, please choose to feel my love; if you ever feel scared or lonely. Please choose to protect yourself. Always pray and seek God's help, direction, protection and guidance. I will always love you, accept you and believe you.

Love You Forever,

Danette Mahabeer
(Mother)

Printed in the United States
By Bookmasters